John Barbour

TABLE OF CONTENTS

INTRODUCTION

As an almost homeless, parentless six-year-old in Toronto, I had only two dreams: To become a star hockey player like Wally Stanowski of the Toronto Maple Leafs or move to America. Since I did not have the family or the money to continue playing hockey that only left the dream of coming to America.

My heroes then were actors like Jimmy Stewart in *Mr. Smith Goes to Washington* and especially the film's director, Frank Capra. But more than the make-believe America was the real America with its founding fathers, Thomas Jefferson et al and the intellectual founder of an independent America, Thomas Paine, the son of an English shoemaker who wrote *Common Sense*. What a great obvious title for a pamphlet. He sold 50,000 of them and turned all of the money over to George Washington to feed, clothe, and arm Washington's army. Heady stuff for a kid under ten.

My next writer addiction was America's greatest writer, Mark Twain, who also became a bit of a pamphleteer during America's fake Spanish American War, in which 200,000 Filipino civilians were murdered.

So, with a convicted small felon now in the White House, (the first time ever) while LBJ and the Bushes and Biden got away with not being convicted of the greater crime of being War Criminals, I thought I would put this thin book together as sort of a pamphlet, one that might make you both laugh and learn. There is not one opinion in it, unless you consider a great joke an opinion based on fact! Then there are scores of real facts about the current occupant of the White House. I can hopefully and helpfully lead you to these facts, but I can't make you think. As one of America's greatest comics, Bill Hicks, would say, "Enjoy the read and the ride!"-- John Barbour

1.

THE BIGGEST JOKE IN THE WHITE HOUSE

Donald Trump will be turning January 6th into America's July 4th.

He is building his next wall around New Mexico. He doesn't want any more New Mexicans in the country.

Like every president, Trump is going to build a Presidential library that he says will be the biggest and the best. Right now all he has to put in it are stolen top secret documents.

Contrary to what his born-again supporters believe, God does make some mistakes in whom He or She, or the Divine Transgender builds. He was given ears and never listens to anyone!

He is hard of hearing: When Trump had Netanyahu in the Rose Garden some heckler hollered out, "Go fly a kite!" So Trump called for Air Force One, and took Netanyahu for a flyover of DC.
He thought the guy had said, "Go fly a Kike."

2.

THE TORONTO STAR

I f it doesn't run out of paper, they are preparing for Trump's second merry-go-round!

THE
FIRST 5,276 FALSE
THINGS DONALD
TRUMP SAID AS U.S.
PRESIDENT

By Daniel Dale

3.

HIS ONLY APPENDAGE

The reason Trump gropes women's crotches with his hand is because the middle finger is the only appendage that stays hard.

Do you think more people would have voted for Kamala if she had said, "I just love to grab men by their cocks?"

4.

PRESIDENTIAL QUOTES

Franklin D. Roosevelt at the height of the 1930s Great Depression:

"We have nothing to fear but fear itself."

President Eisenhower on leaving his office to JFK in his farewell address and warning in 1963:

"Beware of the rise of the unchecked military-industrial complex which could be a danger to our country."

President John F. Kennedy when evaluating the CIA and the rise of the military industrial complex:

"Those who make peaceful revolution impossible make violent revolution inevitable."

Donald J. Trump running for his first term as president:

"I just grab them by the pussy! You can do anything!"

5.

MUSIC MAN

When John Kennedy was president he said often his favorite song from *Camelot* was Richard Burton singing *Camelot*.

Donald Trump's favorite song from that brilliant musical would have to be the hilarious upbeat truth for him: *Fie On Goodness.*

And at his inauguration the Marine Corps Band should have played, *Hail To The Thief.*

The other day I was listening to my favorite music station and I heard this new group singing, "Dum Dum Dee Dum Dum Dum Dee Dum..." for two whole minutes. The DJ said that it was the groups hoped for new *Hail To The Chief!*

And of course when every night he goes to bed with the flag he hums to himself,

"This Land Is My Land..."

6.

NEWIES BUT GOODIES!

When Truman was in the White House the sign on his desk said, "The buck stops here." The sign on Trump's desk says, "Making the megabucks start here!"

Trump believes he is the second coming. He has not had a good first cumming since Stormy Daniels.

Trump hates cats! They cannot be told what to do. An advisor suggested he get a German shepherd. He said no because it would look too big in the picture. He said instead he's going to get a little French poodle. Because the French will do anything you tell them.

If you think Elon Musk, the wealthiest man in the world, whose ass and feet Trump kiss frequently has no influence over Trump think again. Trump is thinking of painting the White House green.

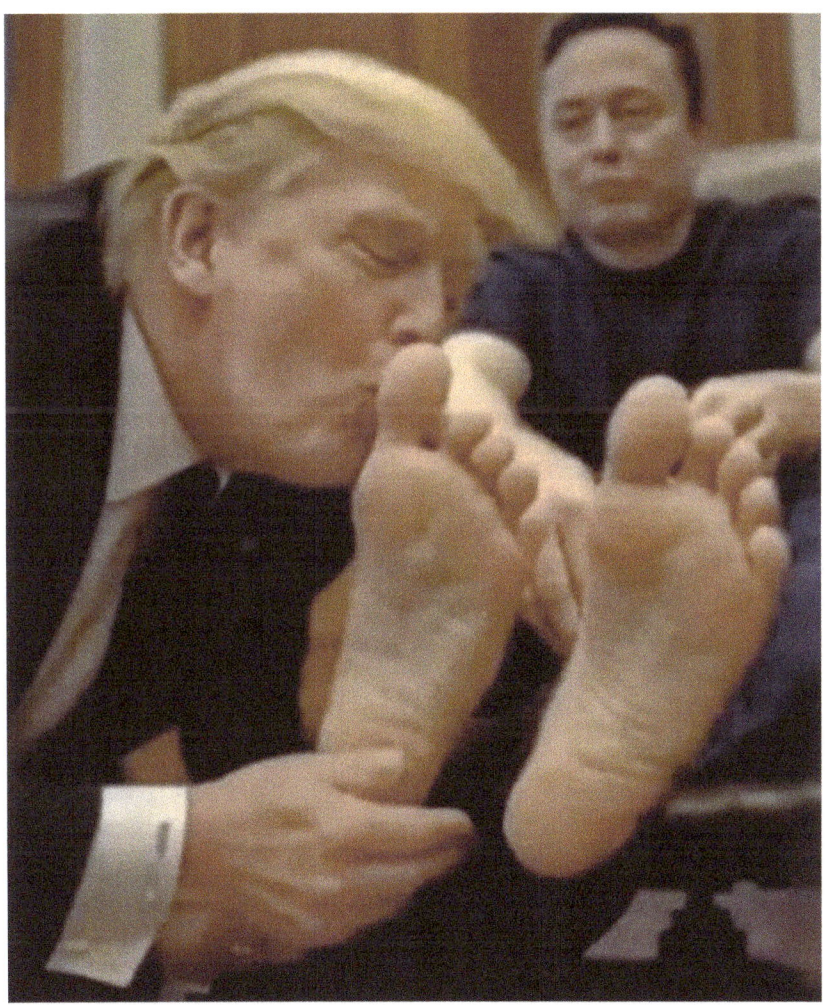

7.

THE FBI'S MAJOR ROLE

The whole country seems to be in an uproar over the fact that Trump is firing thousands of FBI agents, even some who voted for him.

Trashing the FBI should have been done decades ago. They played the major role in the murder of Martin Luther King, Jr. Under code name Zorro, that degenerate fruit cake Hoover called him the most dangerous person in America. When it was actually Hoover who tried to get Dr. King to commit suicide rather than have his infidelities revealed by the press.

The FBI also played a major role in the murder of JFK. And during Lyndon Johnson's and the CIA's fake war on Vietnam, a friend of mine who served in Vietnam said it was safer to be in Vietnam than to march against the war in the United States for fear that some undercover FBI agent might shoot him.

The reason there is no more anti-war movement in the United States: The FBI! At one time in the '50s there were more FBI agents registered in the Socialist Party in order to destroy it from the inside. They also destroyed the meaningful Black Panther movement from the inside committing a number of murders. These are the real reasons the FBI should be dismantled, not because they investigated the January 6th Trump supporting rioters.

8.

A LOUSY SPELLER

Not only was Trump a lousy businessman and already a lousy president, but he is also a lousy speller!

9.

TRUMP OUTDOING CHARLIE BRONSON IN 'DEATH WISH, 2024: REVENGE IS MINE!'

In JFK's inaugural address he said, "Ask not what your country can do for you, but for what you can do for your country." Trump misheard him and thought he said, "What you can do *to* your country." In not one speech did Trump ever say what he was going to do for Americans, but what he and Musk were going to do to Americans.

What they have done in just a couple of short weeks is make DC, which now stands for Different Country, in the USA, which now stands for UnSalvageable America, look like California's Pacific Palisades after the fires.

He is even going after two blind popular podcasters who voted against him. He is taking away their white canes and has assigned South Dakota Governor Kristi Noem, who shot her puppy in the face for not following orders, a task she will love. She is assigned to shoot their seeing-eye dogs.

10.

MORE REVENGE IS SWEET...

Trump's revenge now includes taking over the Kennedy Center after watching part of a gay play that offended him. This makes one wonder if this artistic censoring will discourage Hollywood from making great hilarious films about homosexuality starring Robin Williams called *The Birdcage* and another spectacularly funny film again starring that genius Robin Williams in *Mrs. Doubtfire*. So what will a thin-skinned showman do with an institution central to Washington's cultured life? One expectation is more country music.

11.

DON'T STICK OUT YOUR NECK

The Statue of Liberty is 305 feet high. The inscription most famous on the bottom says, "Give us your poor and huddled masses."

After being deported twice and then finally getting my citizenship papers from California Senator John Tunney when I went to New York to do an entire episode of *Real People*, the first reality show, and one of TV's most successful, which I created about New York, the first thing I did was rush to the lady of liberty and kiss that quote.

Trump hates that quote because he's trying to get millions of immigrants deported. So he asked the French who gave us this great gift to take it back and replace it with another French icon: A 305 foot high replica of the guillotine with the quote, "Don't come here without papers. You'll be sticking your necks out."

If Trump really wants to do something for his country he should pass an executive order to have every major corporation in America with over 15 workers from Google to YouTube to every government agency, to every insurance company or medical company that a human being must answer the phone. This would give wonderful lifelong jobs to the millions he is firing!

12.

TRUMP AND PUTIN: BUDDY, BUDDY!

We now have proof Putin is a liar. He called Trump a genius!

Putin has the same problem with the Ukraine that Trump has with women. Pulling out.

I hate puns, the lowest form of humor, but this describes the lowest form of politicians, if there is such a thing as getting lower than a politician: When Trump went to Moscow to stand and pose for pictures with Putin he stuck an Idaho potato in his crotch. He wanted to show the world that he was indeed the world's biggest dic-tater! (Forgive me.)

When Putin asked Trump what he thought of 9-11, Trump said, "A great store. I just love shopping there."

Trump and his staff would run out of fingers if they were used to telling us the number of his lies. But here is a picture of him showing just five of his worst but his favorites.

1. Having never lived in Michigan he said he was voted Michigan's "Man of the Year!"

2. At the height of the Coronavirus, he said, "I've got it under control. I'm not letting any more Chinese in!"

3. Windmill noises cause cancer.

4. My concept of a health plan will be ready in two weeks.

5. I never gave any money to Stormy Daniels.

13.

WRITTEN BY A PUERTO RICAN

There's a huge pile of human garbage floating around the USA who calls himself President.

USA: Unsalvageable America.

When Trump lost the first election to Biden he blamed Melania. He blames everything on immigrants.

14.

MORE NEWIES BUT GOODIES!

Trump is nothing like JFK or Hitler. They both wrote books!

The presidential plane is now called Hair Force One.

When he flies it, I do not care whether he flies it over the Gulf of Mexico or over the Gulf of America as he wants to call it. As long as he flies it over the Bermuda triangle.

When I look at him, I never think of President's Day. I only think of Halloween. Not because he's more tricks than treats, but he is the color of a pumpkin…orange!

When JFK was president I often thought of him as a Corvette. Every president since him has been an Edsel. And Trump has driven that Edsel into DC and crashed it so badly All the King's Men and all sources can never put it back together again.

You and I now all live in DC: A Different Country.

15.

TRUMP, MUSK, AND VANCE ARE THE REAL RAT PACK!

A nd this to the tune of Frank Sinatra's *My Way* is now *His Way*.

And now your end is near
And so you face your final curtain
You're fired! I'll say it clear
I'll state no reason, 'cuz I'm always certain

But I've lived a life that's full of lying and cheating in every way
Succeeding getting richer because I did It My Way
Regrets, not even one or two. Not even one I'd want to mention
Not even all the bankruptcies I survived without exemption

I planned each tricky course, each crafty step along the byway
Never had more fun doing this. Doing it my way!

Yes there were times, I'm sure you knew

or thought I bit off more than I could chew

But debates and all, when there was doubt I ate up Kamala and spit her out

  I trashed them all and I stood tall and did it my way

I've loved, I've laughed, never cried

I've never had one second of losing

And now as fired losers' tears subside

  I find it all so amusing.

To think I did all that. And may I say in a very proud way

Oh yes, yes it was me

I did it My Way

For what is a president, what has he got, if not in total charge of the country he has naught! There's none in the universe to whom I kneel

So fuck all the fired and what they feel.

The record shows I took the blows the record shows I beat the blows ...

  And did it, yes, morons, and did it...my way!

16.

IF THEY MADE A MOVIE ABOUT TRUMP IT WOULD BE CALLED *COMPULSION*

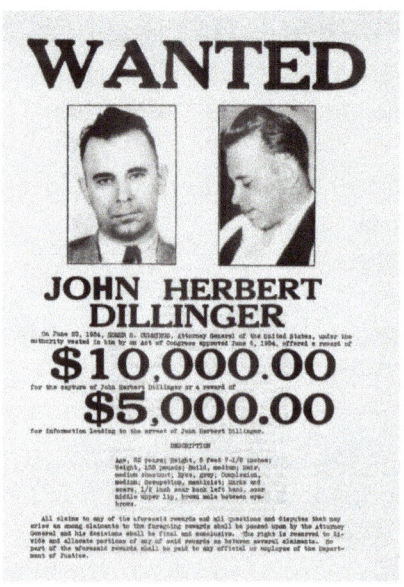

When John Dillinger was America's most notorious bank robber even after he was caught at it, and escaped, he escaped because his compulsion was to rob banks.

Donald Trump's compulsion is to lie. Here he is at a press conference in Paris in late February with President Macron.

Trump is telling the reporters that the French who gave millions to the Ukraine will get a refund. Macron was so disturbed by the untruth of it, he reached over and grabbed Trump by the arm to stop and correct him, saying, "No, no, no. We are not getting any of that aid back." Trump said, "Okay, okay" to him, then turn to the reporters and said, "They're getting their money back, but we are not."

Stopping Donald Trump from lying even after he's caught at it is like stopping Niagara Falls from falling!

17.

REALITY TV

W hen Trump gained popularity as host of *The Apprentice*, it was quite a harmless entertainment reality show and only which one person got fired.

Now that he is President of the United States, he is hosting a monstrously cruel reality show in which, for no clear reason, he is firing millions of people…and gaining even more popularity among some of the millions of morons who voted for him!

Millions of those are devout born again Christians. I am sure if Jesus saw this, he would raise his hands to stop it, and would say, "Forgive him, for he knows not what he does!"

18.

IN A PRESIDENCY LIKE THIS, FREE SPEECH AND COWARDLY SELF-CENSORSHIP GENIUSES ARE WORSE THAN COITUS INTERRUPTUS

One of America's greatest comic strip artists was Gary Larson of the brilliant hilarious sometimes sick, *The Far Side*. He retired years ago at 35, a mega millionaire and still enormously popular.

I bring him up because of what should have been the January 2024 issue of *Vanity Fair* magazine. I find it impossible to look at it and could not imagine that it was a cover not designed solely by Gary Larson. It is genius, with nothing but obvious and simple truths on the left hand side of the page, to the right of a perfect aggressive triumphant looking picture of Trump. That the editors of the once outspoken and daring *Vanity Fair* chose to run for duck and cover, sent me to unsubscribe!

VANITY FAIR

DIGITAL COVER

34
Felony
Counts

1
Conviction

2
Cases
Pending

2
Impeachments

6
Bankruptcies

4
More
Years

The 47th
American
President

19.

DID HE REALLY SAY THAT?

A few of the most moronic things Trump ever said on the campaign trail called by some Native Americans: "The Trail of Tears"!

In Springfield, he said repeatedly, "Haitians are eating the pets of the people that live here." (The pet humane society reported not one incident of one resident missing even a chicken.)

In Atlanta, he said, "Kamala Harris wants to get rid of your cows." (In a city with a population of 510,323 there is not one person who owns a cow.)

In Wisconsin, he said, "107% of all the jobs created by the Biden administration have been taken by immigrants. (Goddamn immigrants. They took 7% more than the maximum!)

In an independent survey, this was deemed the dumbest and most impossible thing he ever said, "If you're young son Jimmy goes to the school, Kamala will supply the funds to have a sex change operation there, and he'll come home a Jane." (This, believe it or not, became the most believed nonsense by the millions of morons who voted for him. Trump is living proof of what America's greatest humorist, HL Mencken said in 1932, when he said, "No one in America ever went broke underestimating the intelligence of the American people." (A sex change operation of a student in school faster than a guy can change a flat tire. Just amazing.)

Honey, as Trump warned, I better get this tire changed quickly so when we get to school we pick up our son Jim instead of a new daughter, Jane.

20.

OUT OF THE MOUTHS OF BABES (SATIRE)

This following conversation took place in grade 7 of a public school in Stockton, California, attended mostly by 12-year-old Latino children.

It was a class on geography. The teacher, a young woman, asked a number of students if they knew what the population of the United States was.

After a dozen of "I don't knows," the teacher said, "Surely someone knows what the population of the United States is." After a long pause, a young man raised his hand. The teacher saw him and said, "Ricardo, do you know what the population of the United States is?" Ricardo said quietly, "Yes, ma'am." And said nothing else.

"Well," the teacher said, "what is it?"

Ricardo said softly, "My mother and father tell me I should not spread rumors."

The teacher, stunned, asked, "How could it be a rumor when it's a fact?"

Ricardo said softly, "It's a rumor I guess because my parents say that all their friends say it all the time."

The teacher, totally perplexed, asks, "Why on Earth are your parents' friends talking about the population of the United States? And what did they say it is?"

After a moment, Ricardo shyly says, "They say, for electing Donald Trump, the population of the United States…is stupid."

Ricardo was the only student in the class to get an A+.

21.

TO DREAM THE IMPOSSIBLE DREAM

Thousands of Americans now want to see Donald Trump on Mount Rushmore…
        and then pushed off!

Others are having fun making replicas of his head in the beach sand.

Then watching the waves wash him away!

The Chinese really knew their stuff. Discovered in an American misfortune cookie:

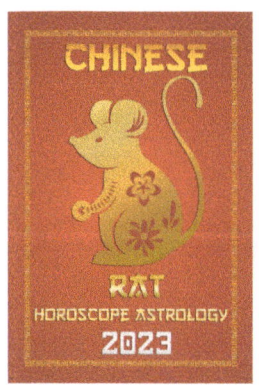

22.

SOMETHING TRUMP MAY WISH HE NEVER SAID

T rump is going around almost quoting Richard Nixon and Napoleon, by saying, "He who saves his country, is not violating the law."

Does this mean that if Thomas Matthew Crooks had been a better shot, in saving America from Trump, he is not violating the law?

23.

ILLUSION OF CHOICE

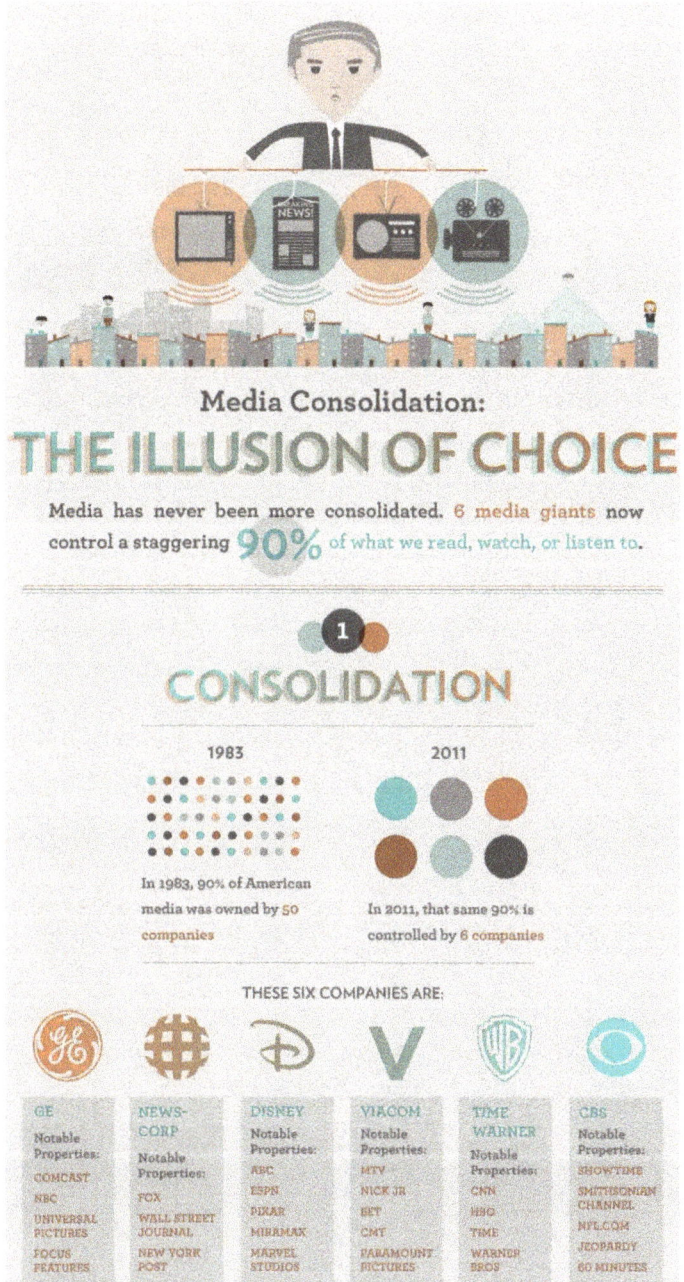

Media Consolidation:

THE ILLUSION OF CHOICE

Media has never been more consolidated. 6 media giants now control a staggering 90% of what we read, watch, or listen to.

1 CONSOLIDATION

1983

In 1983, 90% of American media was owned by 50 companies

2011

In 2011, that same 90% is controlled by 6 companies

THESE SIX COMPANIES ARE:

GE	NEWS-CORP	DISNEY	VIACOM	TIME WARNER	CBS
Notable Properties:		Notable Properties:	Notable Properties:		Notable Properties:
COMCAST	Notable Properties:	ABC	MTV	Notable Properties:	SHOWTIME
NBC	FOX	ESPN	NICK JR	CNN	SMITHSONIAN CHANNEL
UNIVERSAL PICTURES	WALL STREET JOURNAL	PIXAR	BET	HBO	NFL.COM
FOCUS FEATURES	NEW YORK POST	MIRAMAX	CMT	TIME	JEOPARDY
		MARVEL STUDIOS	PARAMOUNT PICTURES	WARNER BROS	60 MINUTES

Bernie Sanders' dire New Year's greeting and warning to Americans after the election of President Musk...oops, Trump, who can no longer do anything about them or the mega billionaires, and the corporations, that own everything in America, corporations that Thomas Jefferson warned us long ago would destroy democracy, is the biggest waste of fucking words that I ever heard from any politician!

He is telling 350 million Americans living paycheck to paycheck or retirement check to retirement check, to unite to retaliate against these oligarchs and the dictator who not only own the country, but a castrated Congress to do something about it. But he doesn't tell us HOW!

How, when Bill Clinton, the biggest sellout and worst president in American history, put all the media into the hands of six corporations so that you and I and the 350 million people have no way to communicate or organize to retaliate, or restore a democracy that is deader than John Kennedy?

If he wanted to say something truthful in wishing us a Happy New Year, he could have just honestly said, ding dong democracy is dead, good luck to the millions and millions of you who are on your own. Or introduce legislation to reverse the communications act which Trump will never do because he loves to call them the fake media. He uses them as a punching bag to regain more power the same way Hitler used Jews in Germany in the '30s, and Joe McCarthy used commies under every bed in the cultural and intellectual and artistic First Amendment destroying 50's!

Sanders is thinking about 350 million Americans, but doesn't know how to talk about it or act on it. Trump, on the other hand, only thinks about himself, which is all he talks about, and as a supreme liar, and convicted criminal now from decades of practice, how to act upon it!

24.

A PENNY STOLEN, IS A PENNY EARNED

To Trump money is not everything…it is the only thing.

25.

TRUMP, SHAKE, RATTLE AND ROLL

This is what happens often to non-Trump voters when he speaks about what he's going to do. They shake their heads to see if they heard him right, rattle their keys to see if they should drive away, or roll their eyes in disbelief. This was one such occasion when he even rattled an unexpected Netanyahu. He said, "We are going to take over the rubble of Gaza, clear it up, and turn it into the Riviera of the Middle East."

Hundreds of outraged and sometimes hilarious comments popped up all over the place. Here is just one that says it all:

Hey, you DT, perfect initials for the guy living in the Trump Tower of Babel, the initials of a drunk. Before Gaza, how about starting with these dirty half dozen: Watts, San Bernardino, and Oakland, where once I lived in a house, then a trailer, now a car. Then St Louis, Detroit, New Orleans, and especially now Murder Bay in DC, made much filthier and more dangerous by your presence. I would say, God help us, but my tank of belief ran out along with the gas in my car!

26.

LIKE PLANTS, PEOPLE ARE KNOWN BY THEIR ROOTS

E ven at 6 when Trump played Monopoly, he always stole the Get Out of Jail Free card.

At 10, his favorite physical activity was jumping up and down on a trampoline. He didn't need to do it with anyone else, and even lied to his father about how high he could jump.

At 13 in school, he paid a fellow student to take his exams. To prove he was superior to that student, he picked the dumbest one in the class.

At 14 he said he had his first and most satisfying sexual experience…with the 14-year-old in the mirror.

At 16, in high school, believe it or not, his hair was already orange, his jacket was orange, and at 18 he knew he had become a man when his face turned orange.

27.

NOT BEING ABLE TO CHANGE ANYTHING DOESN'T MEAN YOU HAVE TO CHANGE YOUR MIND

Common survival sense says if there is nothing you can do about something, you must totally forget about it, and focus on survival and moving forward as best you can. That is exactly what I have to do with my reaction to the law-defying orders being vomited out daily by voted-in President Trump and assigned Co-President Musk.

I have to look at this the same way I look at the weather, which we all can do nothing about. We just have to grin and bear it and learn to live with it. The only difference being, that once in a while, the weather gives us a sunny day.

28.

VENGEANCE IS TRUMP'S

W hen in front of different religious groups, Trump was repeatedly asked what his favorite quotes were from the Bible, and could he name the chapter and verse?

Here is what he said to one group to begin with:

I try to start each day with a little something from the Bible, but I have so much to read, military documents, news articles, legislation, emails from world leaders, I don't often remember if it's Matthew or Luke or whatever.

I especially like that line, "You will have no other Gods before you but me. That's one of my favorites." (Of course it is! Talking about himself!)

With a huge smile, he said, my very very very favorite quote though from the Bible is when the Lord says, Vengence is mine. (He's certainly proving that.)

He said, "One of my other very favorites is that one about the wages of sin is death, but a long life is Jesus. At one of my biggest rallies in the world, a Kamala Commie heckled me saying I was living a life of sin. The crowd wanted to crucify him, but I stopped them and said to him, 'I cannot count one sin I've committed, but whatever I've done I am still counting the wages I've earned from doing it.'

Too bad there were no mics and cameras. Another of the really smart things I always say."

I would bet there were no mics or cameras and that he never said this. In the 50 years since I've been on the Merv Griffin show and watched him, I have only seen vindictiveness, insults, lies, and not one ounce of wit.

I would like to paraphrase Jesus on the cross and say, "Forgive him for he knows not what he does." But the horrifying truth is, he does know!

29.

REGRETS, I'VE HAD A FEW...
(FROM SINATRA'S "MY WAY")

Even though I struggled hard to become an American citizen, deported twice, when I became one, I only voted once. In 1963 when I got my green card, I hoped to vote for JFK in 1964, but the CIA murdered him. I only voted once after that, mistakenly for Obama who I thought would stop the fake wars. Regretting it, two months later I wrote the hilarious The Obama Blues, which is on my website.

Although thousands now say they regret voting for the Trump Musk ticket, I have only one friend who admits it, in a rather heartbroken way. She is an immensely successful entrepreneur and writer. This is how she sat down over a meal she couldn't eat, to tell me why. After listening to her I suggested she post it. She quickly declined, declaring she was afraid for her business and her life. She said even though she kicked me in the balls often for my jokes about Trump, she did manage a laugh or two and would not be bothered if I paraphrased her without identifying her. So simply, this is what she said:

"John, Trump wants to call it the Gulf of America. He wants to call Canada the 51st state.

Historians will one day call his tenure as Captain of this Ship of State, with Musk the navigator, the USS Titanic. It will be sunk by crashing into a massive iceberg of financial greed and even more corruption and lawbreaking. As it sinks, to save themselves, they will lighten the load, by throwing everyone on board into the freezing water of unemployment and hopelessness, which they've already started doing." She paused, her eyes watering, then added, "John, I hope you and your wife and son have a lifeboat to paddle on. Me, I'm going to take a break and do what actor-director Rob Reiner did!"

I asked, "What's that?"

She said, "Commit myself for a few days!"

Which she did.

30.

PROOF THAT TRUTH-TELLERS RUN FOR THEIR
LIVES, WHILE LIARS RUN FOR OFFICE

With all of the pardons granted by Trump to the dozens of proven violent protesters on January 6th, this may be the most offensive. And biggest lie.

As he was entering the Super Bowl game, a journalist almost cornered him asking him why he would grant a pardon to those January 6th offenders who actually were charged with killing a policeman. Which everyone saw on camera.

Trump quickly said, "They didn't attack anyone. The police attacked them," and scurried off.

There was no further comment from that journalist. Or any

other journalist. "Democracy," as JFK said, "does not depend on presidents answering questions. It depends on journalists asking them."

American journalists, because of their fear of the dark shadow being cast over the country by Trump, have been castrated by the cowardice of asking the important questions like, "Mr. President, why haven't you granted a pardon to WikiLeaks founder, Julian Assange, who had to flee the country after pointing out the war crimes committed by the American empire?"

Or, "Mr. President, why haven't you pardoned the CIA employee Ed Snowden, who had to flee the country after pointing out how every citizen was being spied upon by every asset at the government's disposal?"

And, my fellow, trapped Americans, for asking these obvious questions...pardon me!

31.

TO A HUMORIST, TRUMP IS THE GIFT THAT KEEPS ON GIVING

As a dual citizen of Canada and the United States I do not know sometimes whether to be fearful of Trump, or laugh my ass off because he's so fucking stupid!

After he told Trudeau in person that he would still let him be the Governor of the 51st state of the USA, Trump posted this picture of himself standing next to the Canadian flag. But the country he put it in is Switzerland.

Donald J. Trump ✔
@realDonaldTrump

Oh Canada!

From 1939 to 1945, Canada fought valiantly against the Nazis, as much as the Americans. They had no idea they'd have to do it again in 2025!

Canada is one of the most prosperous countries in the world, but if Trump succeeds in taking it over it'll end up like one of his three gambling casinos in Atlantic City.

I live in the gambling capital of the world, Las Vegas, Nevada. No one here has ever gone down the toilet owning any kind of big or little casino. That is an impossibility. If Trump took over the Canadian side of Niagara Falls, it would turn into a dripping faucet.

32.

I CAN LEAD YOU TO THE FACTS BUT I CANNOT MAKE YOU THINK

In the '70s there was a commercial directed at Blacks that said, "a mind is a terrible thing to waste." That commercial should be replayed today for millions who voted for Trump and especially for some of my closest friends. When I ask how could they vote for somebody that's dumber than they are, they just smile and say they like him. Soon I'll point out with American history and common sense, why I believe that is; all based on facts.

In 2016, I predicted he'd win because he wasn't Hillary. Michael Cohen, his 10-year confidant and criminal cohort, who did not escape jail time, said Trump himself was surprised he won. He only ran to publicize his hotels, one of which he hoped to build in Moscow. As a candidate I loved him; he was so freewheeling and entertaining. He is no longer entertaining. As his niece Mary says, he is now dangerous. Now, just a few of the personal and business pesky facts about him, which leads me to my conclusion.

When his father died leaving him 400 million dollars, he hired lawyers to reduce it to a third, depriving his niece of her deserved millions. He fucked her financially. Stormy he fucked for money, other women he groped or raped. Both Mary and

Michael said he had absolutely no feelings for anyone. They pointed out a *New York Times* reporter with palsy, who asked him a question, how Trump answered him by flailing his arms in a deformed fashion. Can you see John Kennedy doing that? Or even a war criminal like Bush? Yet still beloved.

As for his failed businesses, there are too many to count here, but his six bankruptcies deprived thousands employees of their retirement monies. One of his first big mistakes in office in building the promised Mexican wall, pointed out in *60 Minutes*, is how hundreds of yards were built over a river that ran between California and Mexico, There were more Mexicans in it than fish. To tell those inflicted with Covid to drink bleach, showed he knew less about that disease than he did geography. Then he said he could shoot somebody on 5th Avenue and not lose one vote. Then it hit me, why he was and is so beloved and liked, even admired. He is right out of history as one of the greatest most successful con artists and bad guys of all time. As a kid we all saw them in the movies or rooted for them in bestselling books: Billy the Kid. Jesse James. Butch Cassidy. Bonnie and Clyde. John Dillinger. Baby face Nelson. Edward G Robinson. Humphrey Bogart. Jimmy Cagney. We loved the bad guys. And the biggest bad guy in history escaped jail, although being convicted, and lied his way into The White House. He is the only person in the world with the freedom to say: Fuck You! If I don't want to wear a mask, fuck you! If I want to grab someone's pussy, FUCK YOU! If I want to fire or have Musk fire a thousand people, FUCK YOU!

Who would not want that kind of absolute and total freedom with no restraints whatsoever with no consequences. Just being liked even more. What in essence he is saying to Thomas Paine, Thomas Jefferson, Benjamin Franklin, the few presidents who cared about America, the Constitution and the Bill of Rights, and 350 million Americans is FUCK YOU!

With the First Amendment in lockdown, some of us can just post that great *Vanity Fair* cover on the wall and throw darts at it, hoping to spell out F...U...C...K Y...O...U!

33.

TRUMP HAD TO GO TO A PROCTOLOGIST TODAY TO HAVE BOBBY KENNEDY JR'S LIPS REMOVED

With Bobby sucking up to Trump, I am getting scores of notes asking how thrilled I am about the JFK files finally being released. Before I get to that, let me tell you about my experience with Bobby.

It was the 50th anniversary of the murdered John Kennedy. I read that in the Dallas Opera House Bobby told an audience his father did not believe the Warren commission. Enthused by that, I called George Knapp (right), the last great investigative journalist in television, and asked if he would accept $5,000 to interview Bobby if I could get him to come to UNLV to introduce The Garrison Tapes. George said it would be an honor to do it for nothing. Then I called Sean Lawton, now a close friend, who was Bobby's agent at the Kepler agency to find out how much Bobby would charge. Sean  said $25,000. It was my last $25,000, but my wife, Sarita, said okay because it's so important.

Then I called Dick Russell, who writes all of Bobby's

environmental stuff, to see if he would produce the show for $5,000 and act as a go-between between me and Bobby. Dick was thrilled. So I sent a copy of The Garrison Tapes for Bobby to view. Then I contacted the Dean of the Greenwald School of Broadcasting, who thrilled, gave me their largest theater and all equipment free. And a waiting list of 1,200 people. Weeks passed with no word from Bobby and a deadline looming. I called Dick, asking what his friend Bobby thought of the film. Dick said he wouldn't look at it because he thinks Garrison is a kook. At the last minute I had to sadly call the Dean and tell him Bobby was backing out. The Dean quickly said UNLV will pay him an additional $25,000 if he does the interview with George, show your film, then stay an extra day to talk about the environment.

Bobby passed on that also. So much for his desire to learn the truth about the murder of his uncle or even his father. I wrote the greatest and the only fuck you note to him, telling him with my support of Thomas Naguchi (right), the coroner who proved Sirhan standing in front of his father could not have fired the fatal shots, I had done more to help solve the murder of his father than he did. The fatal shots were likely fired by Thane Cesar the security guard at his back, as proven in the

documentary, *The Second Gun*. Cesar immediately retired to the Philippines. A few years later, Cesar told Bobby he would tell him the story for $25,000. Bobby again declined.

But thankfully the dean did not give up. Neither did I. With a smaller theater and facilities free again, I paid Jim Mars, Joan Mellen, and Dick Russell each $1,500, plus enormous expenses to come out and do a Q&A with the audience after the film. It was standing room only.

The film is so powerful I never thought anyone could follow it.

The three of them were so fantastic and could have taken their show to Broadway. The result was the classic historic documentary called *The Last Word on the Assassination*.

Does this sound like a Trump lackey who is interested in seeing the CIA's files released.

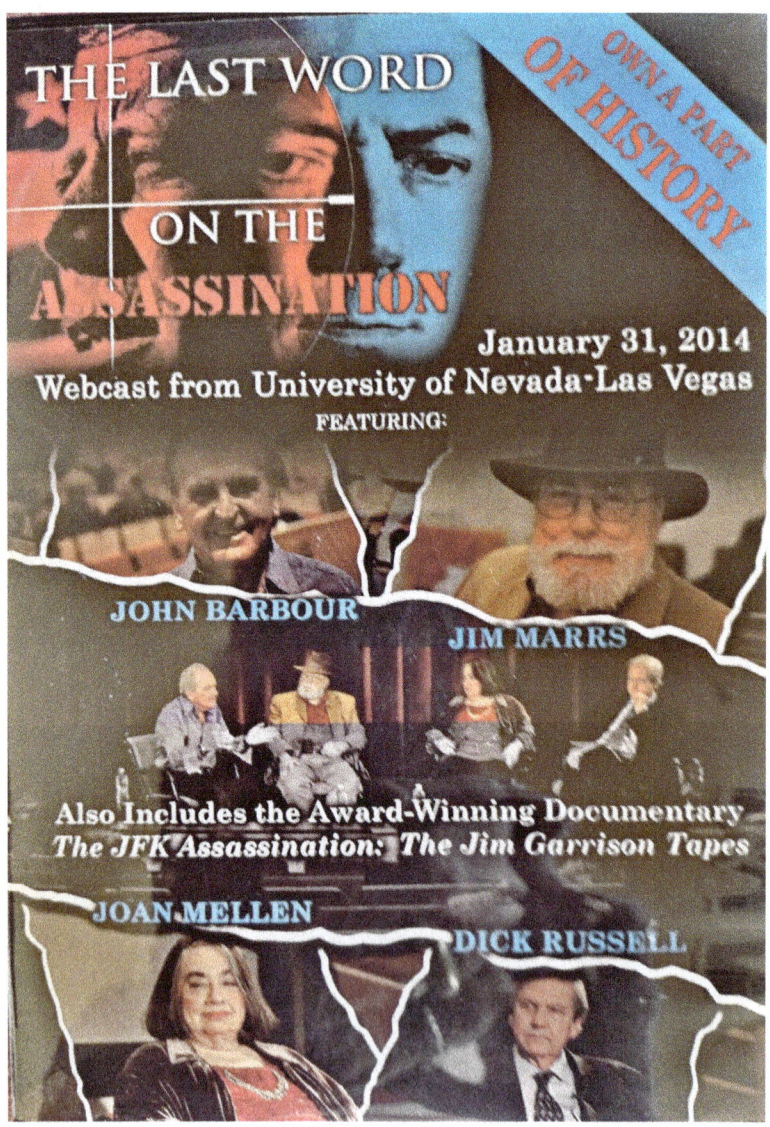

34.

UKRAINE! UKRAINE! UKRAINE! UKRAINE! UKRAINE! OOPS, GAZA!

In all of Trump's speeches and all of the network news, in all of the cable news, and with all the so-called historians, it is endless Ukraine, Ukraine, as the elephant in the room, while that little pesky mouse of Gaza keeps scurrying around out of sight. So right now let's have a little sip of a cup of Truth as Jack Nicholson savagely said in *A Few Good Men*, "You can't handle the truth!" Well let's see if these morons and Donald can.

One of the lies that Biden told us to get us involved in the Ukraine was that according to the NATO treaty if Russia or anyone attacked them, we and NATO had to respond. There is no such treaty. Even if there were treaties, they have never meant anything to America. Just ask a few million Native Americans. 100's broken. Just like the Constitution, which Bush called just a goddamn piece of paper. The costliest broken treaty was the Geneva Accords in the '50s. Under these every country in the world was to stand back and watch North Vietnamese and South Vietnamese vote to see if they wanted to have one country, which would probably be ruled by Ho chi Minh, a Commie. Ike said fuck no and sent in 1200 advisors to stop the election. JFK said hell no to them, and that they'd all be withdrawn by the '64 election.

The CIA said, fuck no to JFK with snipers in Dallas, so he'd never see the '64 election.

Since then in all the NATO countries surrounding Russia, the US has placed missiles aimed at Russia. Russia did not want the Ukraine to become part of NATO and part of another launching pad. 1992 the Ukraine was a major part of Russia, so they decided to reclaim it by sadly brutally invading it. But that is none of our business. When we murdered Allende in Chile, and destroyed Chavez in Venezuela, and destroyed half a dozen other countries in Latin America to prevent them from becoming socialist countries, Russia said not one word. They minded their own business on their side of the planet. We should stick to minding ours. Now to that pesky little mouse: Gaza.

In the thirties, 35 million of the most highly educated people in the world built ovens in which to turn Jews into smoke. When it was over half of Germany went to Russia, the other half should have gone to the surviving Jews. But America and especially England did not want that. They looked back and saw that 5,000 years ago a handful of Jews lived in Palestine as refugees from the pogroms in Egypt. So that's where England and a handful of wealthy Zionists planned to build a country called Israel, a homeland for all the world's Jews. But when they got there they wanted more land, land that was not theirs. First they built barbed wire fences, turning the place into a Middle East Attica prison. Then they invaded the trapped Palestinians with billions in arms supplied by Biden and now by Trump, the Palestinians fighting back with the terrorist weapons of sticks and stones. Trump welcomed the world's greatest child killer and genocidal war criminal to the White House and to speak to Congress, which was as silent as a cockroach. Netanyahu has a specific program for murdering Gaza's children. He calls it "mowing the lawn." He implements it every few years, gloating over the fact that these severed blades of young grass will never grow up. Israel is the only country in the world now without defined borders. It has never signed the anti-nuclear proliferation pact. As I type, Netanyahu is driving the few remaining Gazans into the sea for the natural gas. He is driving them into early graves for their property. And into foreign countries who have all turned them down, just like those countries once did to the Jews.

This is not a war in Palestine. As comedian Bill Hicks said about Iraq, "A war is when each side has an army. This is just target practice."

Scholars and philosophers say we learn from history. Truthfully, what is it that human beings are really learning from history? How to be more evil? How to be greedier? How to kill their fellow human beings more efficiently? How to feel nothing? See nothing. Say nothing. How to bury their heads and hearts into the sand to avoid truth? Or...how to become bigger Morons!

35.

DONALD TRUMP HAS A HARD-ON FOR GAYS!

I mentioned previously one of the reasons he took over as head of the Kennedy Center is that he was offended by some kind of gay show that played there earlier.

I pointed out that I hoped this talent censoring would not inhibit Hollywood from making truly entertaining films about gays like *Birdcage* or Robin Williams dressing as a woman to get a job as a babysitter in the truly funny *Mrs. Doubtfire.*

Now, though, after what he just did to one of the greatest pieces of American history is so fucking pathologically hilarious, which I'll get to in a minute, I wonder if he will try to stop our schools from teaching about the accomplishments of Leonardo da Vinci and Michelangelo, and the Greek philosophers Socrates Plato and Aristotle, all butt bumpers!

BUT...here is the most offensive unbelievable thing this intellectually challenged truth ducking idiot has ever done: Try to alter one of America's most famous or infamous moments. On August the 6th, 1945, to try to end the war with Japan, the United States dropped its first unnecessary bomb on Hiroshima. The plane that dropped it was called *Enola Gay!* Trump has ordered that plane to be  trashed or any reference to its name deleted anywhere and everywhere. And then like a madman possessed, went through the entire list of every service man in America to look for those whose last name was Gay. He found one. An officer yet! And ordered his picture removed. I am 91 and I wear great jockey shorts, but at moments like the above I find I'm laughing so hard sometimes at him and his lies and blunders, that now when I watch him I wear Pampers so I don't piss myself too badly.

By the way, in Springfield, why do the chickens cross the street?

So they won't be eaten by Haitians!

36.

THE CIA-JFK FILES SHELL GAME: FIRST YOU SEE THEM, THEN YOU DON'T!

I n his first go-round with the brass ring in the White House, Trump did a ten-hour interview with journalist Bob Woodward. At one point Woodward confided in Trump that he felt embarrassed having lived most of his lucky life in a cave of privilege that ordinary citizens could 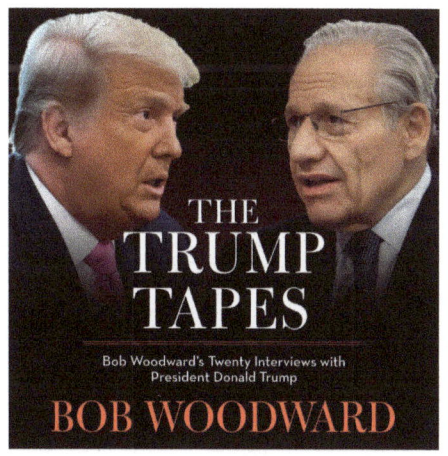 never know. Trump laughed at him and said, "You drank the Kool-Aid. I have never felt like that!"

There you have it right out of his own mouth, as his criminal cohort Michael Cohen and niece Mary say about him. He has no empathy for anyone. But to a con artist, and indeed he is the most successful con artist in American history lying his way all the way into the White House, he is the consummate conman not having empathy for anyone or any convictions about anything, which is an asset. It frees them to lie to the victims he is hustling. And the victims he was hustling and lying to on his way to the White House were us. Since the murder of John Kennedy, to the millions of Americans born and unborn, one of the most important things they wanted to hear about was the release of all the JFK files as mandated by Congress about the murder of John Kennedy. In his first go-round he promised to do that, but did not. At the time, for over five years researcher Jefferson Morley was going through the courts to get not CIA files released but those of Jim Garrison. He finally got a hearing in the highest court

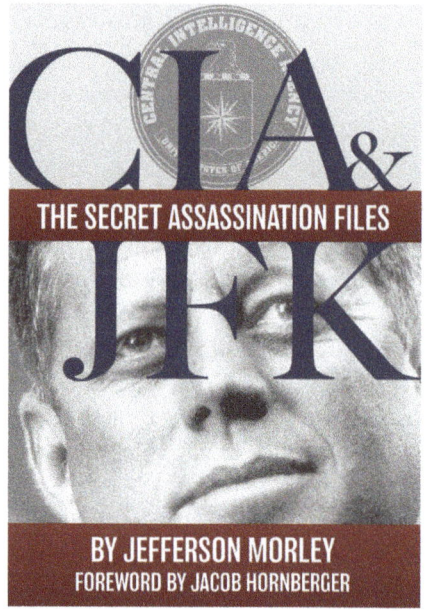

in Washington presided over by rumored sex offender Brett Kavanaugh. Kavanaugh quickly ruled in favor of the CIA never releasing any files. Ever. Trump quickly appointed him to the Supreme Court. Does that sound like a president who wants us to see those CIA files? Even though this time around he says he has signed an Executive Order to have them released, we may have a better chance of seeing his full tax returns first! As they used to say in the movies, "This is a preview of coming attractions."

37.

THERE'S NO BUSINESS LIKE SHOW...ME WHAT'S LEFT OF TRUMP'S BUSINESSES

In his second go round at trying to be a president, has Trump brought with him the inability to run the really big business that is the United States, that the record showed he displayed in trying to run a bunch of smaller businesses?

He said the first smart business thing he was going to do was impose tariffs on Canada and Mexico. In minutes, an $80,000 truck went up immediately to a $100,000 truck. The next day the market had its worse crash in decades. He was forced to cancel the tariffs, which did not last as long as his sex with Stormy Daniels.

Some of Trump's private business failures:

Six bankruptcies, which include four huge gambling casinos where it is almost impossible to lose a nickel.

A few of Trump's failed businesses: Trump's steaks, university, vodka, ice and charities, for which the attorney general fined him $2 million for what else? Lying! Plus a lost lawsuit for racial discrimination in real estate. He's had more business failings than the moral failings of pussy grabbing, which also ended up as losses in court.

In the short, while he and Co-President Musk were in office, it was almost as impossible to find one positive thing they have done, in what is now a huge political garbage can, as it is for a homeless person to find a scrap of food in a smaller garbage can.

38.

TRUMP SIGNS THE WRONG EXECUTIVE ORDERS

Because of Trump's closeness to Stone and Cohen and knowing how corrupt 95% of all congressmen, senators, Wall Street bankers are, and he himself is, my feeling is he must know the CIA murdered John Kennedy. One of the first things he did this time in office was sign an Executive Order to release all the files, exciting millions of us; a month in we've seen none. Sometimes I have the feeling he is not too enthused about releasing them because that would be a bigger story than he is. But there was no need to sign that Executive Order. The murders of John Kennedy and Martin Luther King, Jr. are already cold cases in the Justice Department as conspiracies, put there by the House Select Committee for further investigation. All Trump had to do was tell Justice to reopen it as ordered. He did not. If he deeply felt or knew the CIA murdered JFK, instead of just pardoning January 6th rioters, some who killed a cop, he should have pardoned Lee Harvey Oswald who killed no one. And James Earl Ray who did not kill Dr. King. And then pardon Sirhan who did not kill Bobby Kennedy, as proven by Dr. Noguchi's autopsy in the brilliant documentary *The Second Gun.*

Malice In Wonderland. It gets curiouser and curiouser and interestinger and interestinger!

39.

THE PLOT TO KILL THE KING.
NOT TRUMP. NOT YET.

I n my lifetime I have been lucky enough to meet the two greatest men in America who truly risked everything to do as President Kennedy asked, "Something for your country."

First, Jim Garrison, the New Orleans DA, who on his deathbed chose me over Oliver Stone to be his Boswell to tell his solved sabotaged investigation into the murder of John Kennedy in the two most definitive historic documentaries. The other is William F. Pepper (right, with Martin Luther King, Jr.), author of *The Plot to Kill the King*. Not only did he solve the murder of Dr. King, who did not die from the gunshot wound, but also lunched with the named

shooter, a Memphis cop whose shot to the chin was enough to get him to the hospital, where it was pre-planned by the lead doctor that he would not leave alive.

William Pepper was also on his deathbed months ago when I decided, along with Len Osanic, William's closest friend, and genius host of Black Op Radio. The result is on YouTube: *The Greatest Piece of Investigative Journalism In 75 Years*. We called it that because no one knew who Pepper was. And late in 2024 it won Andrew Krieg's (President of CAPA) First Whistleblowers Film Festival Award! Here are three important things you should know about William Pepper:

It was Dr. King who came looking for him after William as a young photojournalist ran a series of pictures in Ramparts magazine about America's napalm incinerating Vietnamese children.

In Tennessee he won a major judgment against the US

government on behalf of Coretta King for their involvement in the murder of her husband. She could have asked for millions. She only asked for $1,000 burial expenses.

Pepper represented Sirhan at his last denied parole hearings, in which he proved Sirhan was not the killer. The head of the parole board just told Pepper Sirhan was now considered a political prisoner.

Trump should be looking at this film, where he doesn't have to struggle to turn a page reading Roger Stone's nonsense about LBJ. That Trump was inaugurated on Martin Luther King, Jr.'s birthday shows that the gods or God has a really sick, sick sense of humor.

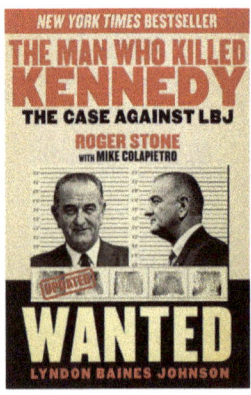

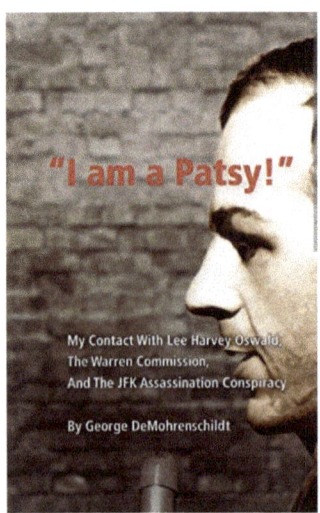

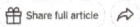

Board Denies Parole for Sirhan Sirhan, the Assassin of Robert F. Kennedy

The California parole board reversed course from its 2021 recommendation that Mr. Sirhan be released from prison. That decision was rejected by Gov. Gavin Newsom.

🎁 Share full article   ↪   🔖

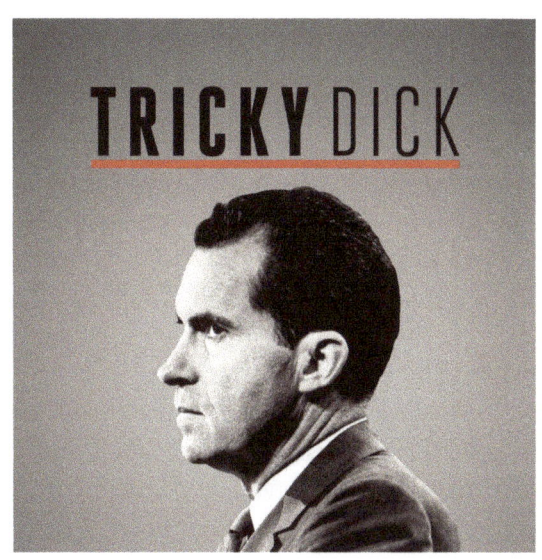

40.

"LET JUSTICE BE DONE THOUGH THE HEAVENS FALL"

The inscription on Jim Garrison's (right) tombstone keeps alive in me the need to keep telling his story to a blacked out America. When Trump took office the second time, one of the first things he said was that he was signing an executive order to release all the CIA files. Millions of Americans and a few in the major media were jumping up and down in praise of him and of Bobby Kennedy, Jr., who many felt encouraged Trump to do that, knowing that's what millions wanted to hear. What they never heard once was the name Jim Garrison, the only law enforcement officer to actually investigate and solve the case. And he solved it simply with basic CSI detective work, which of course the Warren Commission did not want to do because they were assigned to first stop the murder investigation in Texas, and to stop it on a national level with the help of a few "Honorable Men" headed by Chief Justice Earl Warren. The most honorable. (They are all "Honorable Men" said Marc Antony in Julius Caesar.)

Aside from easily finding out Oswald's, Ferrie's and Shaw's involvement in the CIA, through tax records, he just as easily discovered who gave the orders to Ruby to shoot Oswald. Lawrence V. Meyers. He gathered all the above phone records for three months, which led to a hotel room in Chicago where the mistress of Lawrence V. Myers lived. Meyers was a successful businessman and Mafia associate. In the Warren report itself, Garrison then read unbelievably that the day before Ruby shot Oswald he dined with Myers at the Cabana. Bingo.

Now, most really good researchers think it was Allen Dulles head of the CIA, and fired by JFK after the disastrous Bay of Pigs, who was responsible for JFK's murder. He was not. He was just the engineer, hireling of the oligarchs.

When interviewing Garrison on September 5th, 1981 for over 3 hours, a few times he had me turn off the cameras

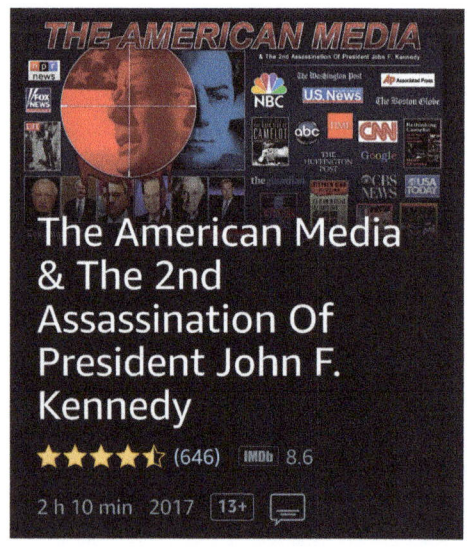

The American Media & The 2nd Assassination Of President John F. Kennedy

★★★★½ (646) IMDb 8.6

2 h 10 min 2017 13+

because he did not want to speculate for the record. Off the record he said he had enough actual and circumstantial evidence to tell me the kill order was given by Avril Harriman, one of the billionaire oligarchs, and military advisor to President Kennedy, placed there to keep an eye on him. Harriman wanted more of Ike's advisors sent to Vietnam. JFK said publicly there will be no Americans there after 1964. That is when Harriman told Dulles to off him before '64. Garrison said Harriman began with Cable 243 in which Harriman ordered Henry Cabot Lodge and the CIA to first off Diem in Vietnam. Sent without either JFK or Bobby Kennedy knowing about it. When Bobby did discover it, it resulted in an actual fist fight, after which Harriman said to the New York Times the Kennedy brothers are nuts. Less than 30 days later JFK was offed in Dallas.

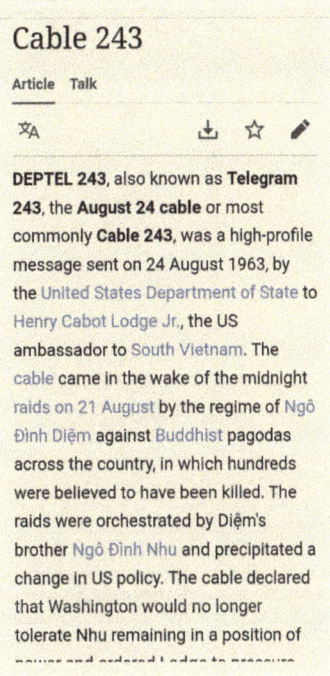

Cable 243

Article Talk

文A   ⬇ ☆ ✎

DEPTEL 243, also known as **Telegram 243**, the **August 24 cable** or most commonly **Cable 243**, was a high-profile message sent on 24 August 1963, by the United States Department of State to Henry Cabot Lodge Jr., the US ambassador to South Vietnam. The cable came in the wake of the midnight raids on 21 August by the regime of Ngô Đình Diệm against Buddhist pagodas across the country, in which hundreds were believed to have been killed. The raids were orchestrated by Diệm's brother Ngô Đình Nhu and precipitated a change in US policy. The cable declared that Washington would no longer tolerate Nhu remaining in a position of

If Cuba was the Bay of Pigs, ever since November 23rd, 1963, DC has been the City of Pigs.

Millions who voted for Trump hoped he would get rid of the Deep State. Garrison said then, there is no Deep State. It is now the above board United States until the people do something about the murder of their President John F. Kennedy!

Those who worry about Trump, need not. He is perfect for the handful of oligarchs that actually own this country. His know-nothing-fire-everybody antics, and deport even some citizens, keeps us (USA: US Apart) so divided, the oligarchs can get more laws passed and more freedoms denied us to control us.

During the Vietnam War many cynics used to say put it on ABC TV and it'll be canceled in 13 weeks. It makes one wonder if Trump's nation-wrecking new reality show will last four years. Or as he predicts and is planning...longer for the Trump family to be around in America as long as the Borgias were in Italy!

41.

NOT JUST A COUNTRY WRECKER, BUT A HOME WRECKER

Trump is trying his inept best at outdoing Clinton as the worst president in American history; charming Billy who signed NAFTA, sending jobs overseas, repealing FDR's Glass-Steagall Act, harnessing Wall Street, then signing the Communications Act, putting all our media in the hands of six corporations. But he did something worse.

After the CIA murdered John Kennedy, we had a number of godawful presidents: Nixon who destroyed Chile. LBJ who destroyed Vietnam. Bush Sr. starting the first Gulf War. Bush Jr. who destroyed Iraq. Obama destroying Libya. war criminals all.

Regardless of the millions of Americans who applauded these war criminals, I never knew of one marriage or one friendship that was destroyed by admirers of these criminals. But that was not the case with Trump. Only he could do that

And that was to destroy human relationships. Husbands and wives divorced. Brothers never speaking to one another. Children not speaking to parents. Business partners parting. Deep lifelong friendships destroyed. I knew many. As do you.

42.

A LIGHT OF HOPE

This iconic picture to me is both heartbreaking and hopeful. Taken during the Cuban Missile Crisis the two close brothers, alone, are trying to think of a way to avoid a possible nuclear holocaust with Russia. Fortunately for mankind they succeeded. They are in silhouetted darkness, like the darkness of the hearts of the men who murdered them. But for the brief time they were here, they were the shining light of hope. A light of hope that still shines for me and millions of Americans. But a light that is dimming in this once bright land. The threat to America no longer comes from Russia, but from the White House and its unqualified occupant, the reason for, and the sad inspiration for this book.

ACKNOWLEDGEMENTS

To me these are more than just four acknowledgments. They are deep, heartfelt thanks and gratitude.

First to Karl Tate, an absolutely brilliant original creative graphic artist, who not only designed two of my previous books, from the great artwork of the covers to the formatting of the pages, making them beautiful and a must read, as hopefully some of the content.

Carol Hoenig. Without Carol my previous books, from my 752-page autobiography, *Your Mother's Not a Virgin*, to this latest work would not exist. On her own, she is a successful author of a number of great novels, and I have met no one else who as a writer cherishes the words of the Constitution and Bill of Rights written primarily by Thomas Jefferson, more than she does; the writing that became the foundation of this country. She once asked me why I didn't try writing fiction. I said I have no imagination and reality keeps getting in the way.

For over five years, this amazing woman and talent set aside her own writing of fiction to help me continue writing and compiling my views on reality.

Christopher Barbour. Sarita's and my son is one of three geniuses that I've ever met. The other two are Jim Garrison and scientist Buckminster Fuller. My autobiography is filled with great stories about him. And from child to man, my heart overflows with love for him. His unselfish financial support has not only made many of my large expensive films possible, but also this little, to me and hopefully others, much needed book.

Sarita Barbour, my wife, companion, inspiration, support, partner, and cohort since November 1963. Without her there would have been no Christopher, no "Real People," the first reality show, and one of the most successful and original in TV history. And no Garrison Tapes. And not even this little book. I spend hours and hours and days and days wrapped up in my films and writing, some which cost us a lot of money. She never once complains. She just asks, "How much do you need?" When I ask her why doesn't she complain once in a while, she says simply, "The world needs to see your films and your words, because nobody else can show it and say it like you, my husband."

Woody Allen recently said everything in life is a matter of good luck. He is right. And I am living with her!